CONTENTS

BRAN BAKED FISH

MAKES 6 SERVINGS | PREP TIME: 25 minutes **TOTAL TIME:** 45 minutes

1¾ cups *Kellogg's® All-Bran®* Original Cereal

½ teaspoon garlic powder

½ teaspoon basil leaves

½ teaspoon grated lemon peel

1 teaspoon grated Parmesan cheese

2 tablespoons margarine or butter, melted

½ cup low-fat plain yogurt

¼ teaspoon salt

⅛ teaspoon pepper

2 tablespoons lemon juice

2 tablespoons ketchup

1 pound frozen or fresh perch fish fillets, thawed and drained

1 tablespoon chopped parsley

1 In electric blender or food processor, crush KELLOGG'S ALL-BRAN cereal into fine crumbs. Add garlic powder, basil, lemon peel, cheese and margarine. Place in shallow pan or plate. Set aside.

2 In small bowl, combine yogurt, salt, pepper, lemon juice and ketchup. Coat fish with yogurt mixture then, cereal mixture, covering completely. Place in single layer, on shallow baking pan coated with cooking spray or foil-lined.

3 Bake at 375°F about 10 minutes. Turn fish. Bake 10 minutes longer or until fish flakes. Serve hot, garnished with chopped parsley.

BRAN NUT BREAD

MAKES 1 LOAF (16 SERVINGS PER LOAF)

PREP TIME: 20 minutes **TOTAL TIME:** 2 hours 20 minutes

2 cups all-purpose flour

½ cup sugar

1 teaspoon baking powder

½ teaspoon baking soda

½ teaspoon salt

1½ cups *Kellogg's® All-Bran®* Original Cereal

1⅓ cups milk

2 eggs

½ cup shortening

½ cup chopped nuts

1 Stir together flour, sugar, baking powder, baking soda and salt. Set aside.

2 In large mixing bowl, combine KELLOGG'S ALL-BRAN cereal and milk. Let stand about 2 minutes or until cereal softens. Add eggs and shortening. Beat well. Stir in nuts. Add flour mixture, stirring only until combined. Spread evenly in 9×5×3-inch loaf pan coated with cooking spray.

3 Bake at 350°F about 1 hour or until wooden pick inserted near center comes out clean. Cool 10 minutes before removing from pan. Cool completely on wire rack before slicing.

VARIATIONS

BRAN BANANA BREAD: Substitute 1½ cups mashed, ripe bananas (about 3) for the 1½ cups milk.

CHERRY-TOPPED BREAD: Finely chop contents of one 10-ounce jar maraschino cherries, drained. Stir 2 tablespoons of the cherries into batter with nuts. For topping, combine remaining cherries with 1 tablespoon melted margarine or butter, ¼ cup sugar and ¼ cup chopped nuts. Sprinkle over batter before baking.

SPICY APPLESAUCE BREAD: Stir 1 teaspoon cinnamon and ½ teaspoon nutmeg into flour mixture. Substitute 1½ cups applesauce for the 1⅓ cups milk.

SAVORY CARAWAY-ONION BREAD: Omit nuts and decrease sugar to ¼ cup. Add 2 teaspoons caraway seeds to flour mixture. Cook ½ cup finely chopped onions in 2 tablespoons margarine or butter until tender. Stir into cereal-milk mixture.

BACK-TO-BASICS BREAD: Substitute ¾ cup whole wheat flour and 1 cup all-purpose flour for the 2 cups all-purpose flour. Substitute ⅓ cup firmly packed brown sugar for the ½ cup granulated sugar.

RAISIN-RICK BREAD: Stir ½ cup seedless raisins into batter with nuts.

CHOCOLATE SCOTCHEROOS

MAKES 24 SERVINGS | PREP TIME: 20 minutes **TOTAL TIME:** 1 hour 20 minutes

1 cup light corn syrup

1 cup sugar

1 cup creamy peanut butter

6 cups *Kellogg's® Rice Krispies® Cereal* or *Kellogg's® Cocoa Krispies®* Cereal

1 cup semi-sweet chocolate chips (6 ounces)

1 cup butterscotch chips

1 Place corn syrup and sugar into 3-quart saucepan. Cook over medium heat, stirring frequently, until sugar dissolves and mixture begins to boil. Remove from heat. Stir in peanut butter. Mix well. Add KELLOGG'S RICE KRISPIES cereal. Stir until well coated. Evenly press mixture into 13×9×2-inch pan coated with cooking spray. Set aside.

2 Melt chocolate and butterscotch chips together in 1-quart saucepan over low heat, stirring constantly. Spread evenly over cereal mixture. Let stand until firm. Cut into 2×1-inch bars when cool.

COCOA KRISPIES® TREATS

MAKES 12 SERVINGS | PREP TIME: 10 minutes **TOTAL TIME:** 30 minutes

3 tablespoons butter or margarine

1 package (10 ounces, about 40) regular marshmallows or 4 cups miniature marshmallows

6 cups *Kellogg's® Cocoa Krispies®* Cereal

1 In large saucepan, melt butter over low heat. Add marshmallows and stir until completely melted. Remove from heat.

2 Add KELLOGG'S COCOA KRISPIES cereal. Stir until well coated.

3 Using buttered spatula or wax paper evenly press mixture into 13×9×2-inch pan coated with cooking spray. Cool. Cut into 2-inch squares. Best if served the same day.

MICROWAVE DIRECTIONS

In microwave-safe bowl, heat butter and marshmallows on HIGH for 3 minutes, stirring after 2 minutes. Stir until smooth. Follow steps 2 and 3 above. Microwave cooking times may vary.

NOTES

For best results, use fresh marshmallows.

1 jar (7 ounces) marshmallow crème can be substituted for marshmallows.

Diet, reduced calorie or tub margarine is not recommended. Store no more than 2 days at room temperature in airtight container.

To freeze, place in layers separated by wax paper in airtight container. Freeze for up to 6 weeks. Let stand at room temperature for 15 minutes before serving.

CREAMY GREEN BEAN CASSEROLE

MAKES 8 SERVINGS | **PREP TIME:** 20 minutes **TOTAL TIME:** 40 minutes

- ¼ cup margarine or butter, divided
- 2 cups *Kellogg's® Corn Flakes®* Cereal (crushed to 1½ cups)
- 2 tablespoons all-purpose flour
- ¼ teaspoon salt
- ¼ teaspoon pepper
- 1 teaspoon sugar
- 1½ teaspoons onion powder
- 1 cup low-fat sour cream
- 1 (20-ounce) package French-style green beans, cooked and drained
- 1 cup shredded low-fat Swiss cheese (4 ounces)

1 In 3-quart saucepan, melt margarine over low heat. Remove from heat. Remove 2 tablespoons margarine and mix with KELLOGG'S CORN FLAKES cereal. Set aside for topping.

2 To remaining margarine in pan, stir in flour, salt, pepper, sugar and onion powder. Gradually stir in sour cream. Fold in green beans. Pour into 10×6×2-inch (1½-quart) glass baking dish coated with cooking spray. Sprinkle cheese and cereal mixture over casserole.

3 Bake at 400°F about 20 minutes or until thoroughly heated. Serve hot.

CRISPY FRENCH TOAST

MAKES 4 SERVINGS | PREP TIME: 10 minutes **TOTAL TIME:** 10 minutes

2 cups *Kellogg's®* Corn Flake Crumbs or 8 cups *Kellogg's® Corn Flakes®* Cereal (crushed to 2 cups)

2 cups milk

2 eggs

½ cup sugar

1 tablespoon cinnamon

8 slices stale bread

Maple syrup (optional)

1 Place KELLOGG'S CORN FLAKE crumbs in shallow pan. Set aside.

2 In medium bowl, combine milk, eggs, sugar and cinnamon. Dip bread into egg mixture coating both sides of bread. Coat bread with KELLOGG'S CORN FLAKE crumbs.

3 On grill or in large fry pan coated with cooking spray, cook bread on medium heat until both sides are golden brown, turning once. Serve hot with warm maple syrup.

DOUBLE-COATED CHICKEN

7 cups *Kellogg's® Corn Flakes®* Cereal (crushed to 1¾ cups) *or* 1¾ cups *Kellogg's®* Corn Flake Crumbs

1 egg

1 cup fat-free milk

1 cup all-purpose flour

½ teaspoon salt

¼ teaspoon pepper

3 pounds chicken pieces (without or with skin), rinsed and dried

3 tablespoons margarine or butter, melted

1 Place KELLOGG'S CORN FLAKES cereal in shallow dish or pan. Set aside.

2 In medium mixing bowl, beat egg and milk slightly. Add flour, salt and pepper. Mix until smooth. Dip chicken in batter. Coat with cereal. Place in single layer, in shallow baking pan coated with cooking spray or foil-lined. Drizzle with margarine.

3 Bake at 350°F about 1 hour or until chicken is tender, no longer pink and juices run clear. Do not cover pan or turn chicken while baking. Serve hot.

FAMILY TUNA CASSEROLE

MAKES 6 SERVINGS | **PREP TIME:** 15 minutes **TOTAL TIME:** 45 minutes

1½ cups *Kellogg's® All-Bran® Complete®* Wheat Bran Flakes Cereal, divided

2 teaspoons butter or margarine, melted

1 cup (4 ounces) shredded American cheese, divided

1 can (6½ ounces) chunk light tuna in water, well-drained and flaked

1 can (10½ ounces) condensed cream of mushroom soup

⅓ cup non-fat milk

2 cups egg noodles, cooked and drained

½ cup cooked peas

½ cup thinly sliced celery

2 tablespoons chopped pimientos

1 In small mixing bowl, toss 1 cup KELLOGG'S ALL-BRAN COMPLETE cereal and butter. Set aside for topping. Set aside ½ cup of the cheese.

2 Stir together remaining cereal, remaining cheese, tuna, soup and milk in large mixing bowl. Stir in noodles, peas, celery and pimientos. Spread in 10×6×2-inch (1½-quart) glass baking dish. Sprinkle with cereal topping.

3 Bake at 350°F for 25 minutes. Top with reserved cheese. Bake about 5 minutes longer or until cheese melts and tuna mixture is thoroughly heated.

GOOD AND SPICY MEATBALLS

MAKES 6 SERVINGS | **PREP TIME:** 30 minutes **TOTAL TIME:** 1 hour

2 cups *Kellogg's® Corn Flakes®* Cereal

2 tablespoons ketchup

1 egg, slightly beaten

1 pound lean ground beef

1 (15-ounce) can tomato sauce

½ cup ketchup

¼ cup firmly packed brown sugar

2 tablespoons pickle relish

1 tablespoon Worcestershire sauce

2 teaspoons vinegar

¼ teaspoon pepper

1 In large mixing bowl, combine KELLOGG'S CORN FLAKES cereal, 2 tablespoons ketchup and egg. Mix in ground beef. Shape into 1¼-inch meatballs. Place in single layer, in shallow baking pan coated with cooking spray.

2 Bake at 400°F for 12 minutes or until browned.

3 In 4-quart saucepan, combine remaining ingredients. Simmer over low heat 15 minutes, stirring frequently. Add meatballs. Continue cooking 15 minutes. Serve over rice, if desired.

KELLOGG'S® CORN FLAKES®
BANANA BREAD

MAKES 1 LOAF (16 SLICES PER LOAF)

PREP TIME: 20 minutes **TOTAL TIME:** 1 hour

2 cups all-purpose flour

1 teaspoon baking powder

½ teaspoon baking soda

½ teaspoon salt

1½ cups mashed, ripe bananas

2½ cups *Kellogg's® Corn Flakes®* Cereal

½ cup margarine or butter, softened

¾ cup sugar

2 eggs

½ cup coarsely chopped walnuts

1 Stir together flour, baking powder, baking soda and salt. Set aside.

2 In medium mixing bowl, combine bananas and KELLOGG'S CORN FLAKES cereal. Let stand 5 minutes or until cereal softens. Beat well.

3 In large mixing bowl, beat margarine and sugar until combined. Add eggs. Beat well. Mix in cereal mixture and nuts. Stir in flour mixture. Spread batter evenly in 9×5×3-inch loaf pan coated with cooking spray.

4 Bake at 350°F about 1 hour or until wooden pick inserted near center comes out clean. Let cool 10 minutes before removing from pan. Cool completely before slicing. Wrap with plastic wrap.

KELLOGG'S®
CORN FLAKES® COOKIES

MAKES 30 COOKIES | **PREP TIME:** 30 minutes **TOTAL TIME:** 1 hour

2 cups all-purpose flour

½ teaspoon salt

1 cup butter or margarine, softened

⅔ cup sugar

3 egg yolks

½ teaspoon grated lemon peel

1 teaspoon vanilla extract

2 cups *Kellogg's® Corn Flakes®* Cereal (crushed to ½ cup)

1 Stir together flour and salt. Set aside.

2 In large mixing bowl, beat together butter, sugar, egg yolks, lemon peel and vanilla until well combined. Add flour mixture, mixing well. Portion and shape dough into 1-inch balls. Roll in KELLOGG'S CORN FLAKES cereal. Place on ungreased baking sheets, about 2 inches apart. Flatten slightly.

3 Bake at 375°F about 8 minutes or until edges are lightly browned. Remove from baking sheets and cool on wire racks. Store in airtight container.

SPECIAL K® COOKIES

MAKES 4 DOZEN COOKIES | PREP TIME: 15 minutes **TOTAL TIME:** 25 minutes

4 cups *Kellogg's® Special K®* Cereal Original, crushed to 1½ cups and divided

1 cup all-purpose flour

1 teaspoon baking powder

¼ teaspoon salt

½ cup margarine or butter, softened

⅔ cup sugar

1 egg

1 teaspoon vanilla extract

1 Stir together 1 cup of the crushed KELLOGG'S SPECIAL K cereal, flour, baking powder and salt. Set aside.

2 In large mixing bowl, beat margarine and sugar until light and fluffy. Add egg and vanilla. Beat well. Add flour mixture. Mix until well combined. Portion dough using rounded measuring teaspoon. Shape into balls. Roll in the remaining ½ cup crushed cereal. Place about 2 inches apart on ungreased baking sheets.

3 Bake at 375°F for 10 minutes or until lightly browned. Remove immediately from baking sheets. Cool on wire racks.

VARIATIONS

CHOCOLATE: Stir in ½ cup semi-sweet chocolate chips with the KELLOGG'S SPECIAL K cereal.

COCONUT: Stir in ½ cup shredded coconut with the KELLOGG'S SPECIAL K cereal.

DATE: Stir in ½ cup cut dates with the KELLOGG'S SPECIAL K cereal.

THE ORIGINAL
RICE KRISPIES® TREATS

MAKES 12 SERVINGS | **PREP TIME:** 10 minutes **TOTAL TIME:** 30 minutes

3 tablespoons margarine or butter

1 package (10 ounces, about 40) regular marshmallows or
4 cups miniature marshmallows

6 cups *Kellogg's® Rice Krispies®* Cereal

1 In large saucepan, melt margarine over low heat. Add marshmallows and stir until completely melted. Remove from heat.

2 Add KELLOGG'S RICE KRISPIES cereal. Stir until well coated.

3 Using buttered spatula or wax paper, evenly press mixture evenly into 13×9×2-inch pan coated with cooking spray. Cut into 2-inch squares when cool. Best if served the same day. Store no more than 2 days in airtight container.

MICROWAVE DIRECTIONS

In microwave-safe bowl, heat margarine and marshmallows on HIGH for 3 minutes, stirring after 2 minutes. Stir until smooth. Follow steps 2 and 3 above. Microwave cooking times may vary.

NOTES

For best results, use fresh marshmallows.

1 jar (7 ounces) marshmallow crème can be substituted for marshmallows.

Diet, reduced calorie or tub margarine is not recommended. Store no more than 2 days at room temperature in airtight container.

To freeze, place in layers separated by wax paper in airtight container. Freeze for up to 6 weeks. Let stand at room temperature for 15 minutes before serving.

SPECIAL K® PARFAIT

MAKES 2 SERVINGS | **PREP TIME:** 5 minutes **TOTAL TIME:** 5 minutes

1 (8-ounce) container low-fat vanilla flavored yogurt

1 cup fresh fruit (sliced strawberries, sliced banana, blueberries or raspberries)

1 cup *Kellogg's® Special K®* Cereal Original

1 In 2 tall glasses, layer yogurt, fruit and SPECIAL K cereal until glass is full.

2 Top with extra fruit.

3 Serve immediately.